D1572198

OTHER BOOKS BY FULTON J. SHEEN

God and Intelligence
Religion Without God
The Life of All Living
Moods and Truths
Old Errors and New Labels
The Divine Romance
The Eternal Galilean
The Seven Last Words
The Mystical Body of Christ
The Philosophy of Science
Calvary and the Mass
The Lord's Prayer on the Cross
The Way of the Cross
The Queen of the Seven Swords
The Cross and the Beatitudes
The Moral Universe
The Tactics of Communism
Liberty Under Communism
Communism Answers Questions of a Communist
Communism and Religion
Communism the Opium of the People
The Rainbow of Sorrow
The Way of the Cross for Our Enemies
The Cross and the Crisis
Liberty, Equality, and Fraternity
Victory Over Vice
Freedom Under God
Whence Come Wars?
The Seven Virtues
For God and Country
A Declaration of Dependence
God and War
Peace
The Armor of God
The Divine Verdict
Philosophies at War
Seven Words to the Cross

Seven Pillars of Peace

Seven Pillars
of Peace

FULTON J. SHEEN

NEW YORK

Charles Scribner's Sons

1944

DEDICATED

TO

MARY IMMACULATE

GRACIOUS MOTHER

OF

DIVINE GRACE

IN TOKEN

OF

LOVE AND GRATITUDE

Preface

AFTER THE Treaty of Amiens in 1802 Napoleon 1 said: "What a beautiful fix we are in now: peace has been declared." This lament is true if by peace is understood the mere cessation of hostilities. No peace is true if it is *declared*. It is significant that in the Sermon on the Mount Our Divine Saviour said: "Blessed are the peace-makers." Peace is *made*: it is not declared. Later on, St. Augustine described such peace as the "tranquility of order."

With peace-making rather than peace-declaring this book is concerned. It challenges the illusions of most planners today that military allies are necessarily political allies; it affirms that a common hatred can make nations *allies*, but only a common love can make them neighbors; it denies the primacy of action over reason, in the sense that the will of the State is that which makes a State right; it contends that utility does not establish justice, but it is justice which makes utility. Every right is useful, but not everything that is useful is right.

On the positive side it lays down seven basic conditions for world peace: (1) The unity of religious groups for social purposes; (2) The primacy of the moral law over force and expediency; (3) The greatest guarantee

9

of economic freedom in the wider diffusion of property; (4) The State exists for the Person, not the Person for the State; (5) The natural unit of national life is the family, not an individual, nor a class; (6) The freedom of people must not be negative but positive; freedom from something is intelligible only in terms of freedom for something; (7) It is not geographical continuity but the recognition of a common moral principle which makes the world one. These are principles, not programs; principles not plans. Because this book deals with foundations of peace rather than with superstructure, it is called *The Seven Pillars of Peace*.

FULTON J. SHEEN

August 5, 1944

Contents

Seven Pillars of Peace

CHAPTER I

The Pillar of Good Will

CENTURIES AGO out over the white chalk hills of Bethlehem there rang a song of angel voices: "Peace on earth to men of good will." Men of good will!

Three times recently we have heard echoes of that song to men of good will. One echo comes from Teheran, the other from the President of the United States, and the third from the Church.

The Conference of Teheran declared: "We recognize fully the supreme responsibility resting upon us and all the nations to make a peace which will command *good will* from the overwhelming masses of the people of the world."

The President of the United States said: "The ninety per cent who want to live in peace under law, and in accordance with moral standards that have received almost universal acceptance through the centuries, can and must find some way to make their will prevail."

Finally, the late Holy Father in addressing "all men of good will" pleaded: "In combating the violence of the powers of darkness . . . we have high hopes that with those who glory in the name of Christian, all those also—and they comprise the great majority of mankind—who believe in God and adore Him, will effectively join."

The Teheran Declaration spoke of "the overwhelming masses of the people of the world" as men of good will; President Roosevelt spoke of their being ninety per cent; and the Holy Father spoke of their comprising "the great majority."

It may appropriately be asked: "If men of good will are the overwhelming majority, why does not good will prevail? The answer of the Holy Father is: "Power is dissipated through disunion."

Men of good will should unite because *there is a common enemy*. "The difficulties, anxieties and trials of the present hour," writes the Pope, "make all believers in God and Christ share the consciousness of a common threat from a common enemy." What is this common enemy? It is the forces that would destroy religion and moral law in favor of power and expediency.

The common enemy has three characteristics: It is atheistic; it is alien to our civilization; and it is a repudiation of the Christian tradition.

Twenty-five years ago atheism was an individual phenomenon; today atheism is social. The atheist who once was a curiosity, is now a component part of some of the governments of the world.

A few decades ago Christianity's struggles were more

in the nature of a civil war; that is, religious rivalries and contentions existed between Methodists and Presbyterians, Lutherans and Anglicans, and in a broader way between Jews, Protestants, and Catholics.

Today that simple condition no longer prevails. Christianity is no longer engaged exclusively in a civil war; it is face to face with an invasion, an incursion of totally alien forces who are opposed to all religion and all morality, whether they be Jewish or Christian. Once men quarreled because they wanted God worshipped in a certain way; now they quarrel because they do not want God worshipped at all. The wars of religion of the seventeenth century have become the wars against religion of the twentieth century.

We live in an age of revolution. But there is a vast difference between the revolutions of our times and those of the past. None of the previous revolutions repudiated the Christian tradition and the moral law. Certainly our American Revolution did not; neither did the English Revolution, nor even the French Revolution. Though there was a spasm of atheism about the French Revolution, its basic principles of liberty, equality, and fraternity were derivatives of Christian thinking.

But the three major revolutions of our times began by repudiating the Christian tradition and the moral law. For the first time in 1900 years, a revolution attempted to seize neither political nor economic wealth, but the souls of men. If these revolutions did look to the past, it was not to a living or historic past, as a man might do who uses his memory; but to a primitive, prehistoric or barbaric past, as a man might do who sought to trace his ancestry to the baboon.

The Fascist Revolution, for example—at least in theory and in principle—skipped nineteen centuries of Christian tradition in Italy, and, for the inspiration of its new order, went back to the Imperialism of Caesar Augustus. The Nazi Revolution blotted out fourteen hundred years of its Christian history and went back to the prehistoric Nordics, to Wotan and the forest nymphs of the Niebelungen saga, whence they sought to derive their Messianic destiny. The Communist Revolution, at least in its beginnings, repudiated a thousand years of Christianity which was so deeply rooted in the Russian soul that the word for peasant and Christian (*krestianin*) were identical. And it gave the Russian people no ties with the past other than those primitive memories of prehistoric cutting and beating, symbolized by a hammer and a sickle. Even in the democracies some individuals and groups were measuring progress by the height of the pile of discarded moral inhibitions, and liberty by the absence of restraint and discipline and the abandonment of Christian morality. This substitution of emotional atavism for spiritual heritages, this amnesia which made men forget the traditions which made them great, has brought us to a day where we fear tomorrow because we have no yesterdays to light the way, and where we act like dull tragedians not knowing what the future holds because we have forgotten the past.

This universal, organized attack upon the moral foundations of society creates a problem. What are men of good will going to do about it? They must unite. There must be a common front against a common affront. The enemy is common to Jews, Protestants, and Catholics. It makes no distinction between them.

The crisis today is not religious, it is cultural. The coming of four-headed Totalitarianism created a new problem, for it divided men not on the basis of their religion, but on the question of whether rights were moral or physical, that is, whether they were God-given or State-given. The new decision which the enemy has forced upon us is: God or anti-God!

The principles which once were taken for granted, because beyond legal controversy or human manipulation, are today challenged. When Thomas Jefferson wrote the Declaration of Independence, he stated it was "self-evident" that man derives his rights and liberties from God, his Creator. When the Catholic Hierarchy paraphrased that statement of Jefferson recently, a back-water press labeled it Fascism. The fact is that what was self-evident to our Founding Fathers, namely, that rights are God-given and not State-given, is not regarded as self-evident today.

The conflict has moved from the domain of the supernatural to the domain of the human; from the higher levels of Christian doctrine to the lower levels of the natural law. The struggle today centers not around belief in the Trinity or Transubstantiation, but around the very minimal moral conditions for preserving even a vestige of civilization. Imagine a Catholic and a Protestant in a forest attempting to settle the problem of Infallibility, not by argument but by muscular Christianity. They are suddenly attacked by a lion. What will they do? They will interrupt their controversy to do battle against their common enemy, of course. In like manner, the forces at work today are animal, demonic, anti-human. The human must assert itself against the anti-human. Never before in the history of Christian civilization has the cause of God and man, of Christianity and Democracy, been as nearly identical as at this very moment. At least faintly, men of good will have realized that the defeat of God is in every instance the defeat of man!

Men of good will must unite! The tragedy of our times is that the moral forces are disunited while the anti-moral forces are united. The State is becoming stronger, more centralized, as the spiritual forces are becoming more disparate. The Jews protest against the persecution of their people and sometimes ignore the persecution of Christians. The Christians protest the persecution of their own people and sometimes ignore the persecution of Jews. It should be elementary that, where basic rights are concerned, men of good will should be united. No man has a right to protest against a persecution unless he condemns it irrespective of where he finds it, and irrespective of who is persecuted. The choosing between totalitarian barbarities has weakened the cause of democracy at the point where it should be strengthened. Some day I hope to see a parade in New York in which Jews will carry banners protesting against the persecution of Christians, accompanied by Christians bearing banners protesting against the persecution of Jews. Persecution is not exclusively anti-Semitic; persecution is not exclusively anti-Christian; persecution is anti-human.

Think not that this plea for unity is born of an admission of weakness, or because I fear that the Church or religion is in danger. Certainly, the Church is not in danger, for it has the divine assurance that Christ will be with it all days even to the consummation of the world. In vain will men look for the death of the undying, or the breaking of the Rock against which even the gates of hell shall not prevail. The Church that survived Neros and Julians, Domitians and barbarian invasions, will also live to sing requiems over Hitler and his fellow-dictators.

It is not the sanctuary that is in danger; it is civilization. It is not infallibility that may go down; it is personal rights. It is not the Eucharist that may pass away; it is freedom of conscience. It is not divine justice that may evaporate; it is the courts of human justice. It is not that God may be driven from His throne; it is that men may lose the meaning of home; it is not that the war may never end; it is that peace may never come. For peace on earth will come only to those who give glory to God! It is not the Church that is in danger, it is the world!

There is greater unity among the forces of evil than among the forces of good. To counteract the common danger there must be greater unity among men of good will. But what kind of unity? As Hamlet said: "Ay! There's the rub."

Shall it be a unity for *religious purposes* or shall it be a unity for *social purposes*? Unity for religious purposes is commonly called union of Churches and holds that the various sects should emerge into common beliefs, rites and forms of worship—broad and vague enough to be acceptable to all. Unity for social purposes, on the contrary, leaves theology untouched and unites religious people rather than religions, on the basis of certain moral principles necessary to guide the political, economic and social life of our times.

Which shall it be? Absolutely not the first, that is, union of Churches on the basis of the widest common denominator. And why not? Well, first of all because it does violence to truth. Religion must begin not by finding out what men want but what God wants. Unity must come not from below, that is, from men, for if the only way we can unite is by scrapping the few divine elements left in common, it would be better to live in isolation. If, as Christ said, "not a single iota" of the truth He gave was to be changed, then by what right do we sit in judgment on Divinity and say: "This much of Your truth we will accept, because it pleases us, and this much we will reject"? We are not the creators of divine truth; we are only the trustees and the guardians. God's truths are not optional any more than the right to happiness is optional; they are not debatable any more than the multiplication table is debatable. Any sect which starts with the assumption that it has rights over God's truth proves that it is man-made, and a religion that is man-made can be man-unmade. But a Church which is God-made cannot be man-unmade.

In rejecting a union of Churches purchased in compromise to truth and history, we pay tribute to the ideals of its advocates who seek to promote charity among all

Christians; but perfect charity is impossible without the fullness of faith. Hence St. John, the great apostle of love, nevertheless forbade association with those who corrupted Christ's teaching: "If any man come to you and bring not this doctrine, receive him not into the house nor say to him: God speed you."

But there is still another kind of unity possible among men of good will, namely, a *unity for social purposes.* Outside of the faith, where we are divided, there is a common ground where cooperation between men of good will is necessary and possible, namely, the preservation of the moral law in the political, economic and international law. For example, we can be united for the defense of private property, for equality to all races, colors and classes, for the betterment of the working classes, for freedom of conscience throughout the world, for a peace based on justice, and for the hundred-and-one other moral requisites of a social order, where men of good will can live short of a risk of martyrdom. It must, however, be understood that cooperation for the preservation of the moral basis of society must never be accepted as a substitute for religion.

There rests an obligation on all Christians to collaborate for the social good. It is easy for us to excuse ourselves from collaboration for social purposes on the grounds that politics are rotten, or that Communists hold important posts in government, or that Capitalism

is incurably selfish, and because of this to draw apart
into a catacombic existence doing nothing except to
chant the lamentations of Jeremiah.

It is incumbent upon us Christians to maintain fel-
lowship across lines of conflict if the moral order of the
world is to survive. This is sound Catholic and Protestant doctrine. When, for example, France was going
through the struggles of monarchy and republicanism,
Leo XIII appealed for joint action of Catholics and non-
Catholics to save the "moral grandeur of France": "We
. . . exhort not only Catholics, but all Frenchmen of
good will and good sense to put far from them every
source of political dissension in order that they may
consecrate their energies solely to the pacification of
their country."

A little later on, Leo XIII gave what he called a
"practical rule," *viz*: "While holding firm to our dog-
matic position and avoiding all compromise with error,
it is Christian prudence not to reject, but rather to win
over to us, the collaboration of all men of good will in
the pursuit of individual and especially of social wel-
fare."

Pius X urged Catholics "to cultivate that peace with
their non-Catholic fellow citizens without which neither
social order nor civil prosperity can be achieved." Let
therefore no Christian excuse himself from the duty of
uniting with men of good will "towards the renewal of

society in spirit and in truth." The present Pope condemned "those currents of thought which hold that since redemption belongs to the sphere of supernatural grace, and is therefore exclusively the work of God, there is no need for us to cooperate on earth. . . . If there ever was an objective deserving the collaboration of all noble and generous minds, if ever there was a spiritual crusade which might assume with a new truth as its motto: 'God wills it,' then it is this high purpose, it is this crusade, *enlisting all unselfish men in all endeavor to lead the nations back from the broken cisterns of material and selfish interests to the living fountain and Divine justice.*"

That shall be the inspiration of this unity. All decent Americans are disturbed by the hate which war engenders; the Jews are worried about anti-Semitism; the Christians are disturbed by the radio commentators and journalists who nine out of ten give approval to those political or world forces which are definitely anti-religious. Up to this time men of good will have attempted to crush this spirit of hate by an appeal for tolerance.

It is our contention that we must find another inspiration for unity because tolerance is inadequate. The reasons are obvious: Modern tolerance has a bad history. It was conceived in its present form by the merchants of the eighteenth century who, seeing that theological disputes hurt trade, suggested that men regard all religion as unimportant: it really made no difference what you believed. Thus tolerance became identified with indifference to truth; right and wrong were regarded as irrelevant points of view. The favorite slogan became: "There are two sides to every question," forgetful that religion, truth and justice, if they had two sides, had them, exactly as flypaper does: the right and wrong. "There are many roads to heaven, it makes no difference which one you take," was another expression of that broadminded era which gave error equal rights with truth, forgetful that the Divine Teacher said there were only two roads: the broad that led to destruction and the narrow that led to life everlasting.

The war has given a terrific jolt to this false tolerance, for if there is no objective difference between right and wrong, independent of our subjective point of view, why should we be fighting the Nazis and the Japs? How could Hitler be wrong and we be right, if it makes no difference what you believe? Nothing has so much vitiated the wells of friendliness as that unspeakably stupid statement of Voltaire about tolerance which is so often quoted: "I disapprove of what you say, but I will defend to the death your right to say it." Now translate that into modern language: Voltaire would say to Hitler: "I disapprove of your saying that Nazism is human and democratic but I will defend to the death your right to say it." Or, "I disapprove of your saying that the President ought to be killed but I will defend to the death your right to say it." ·

And this same Voltaire who set himself up as the apostle of tolerance is the same Voltaire who spent most of his life writing: "Destroy Christianity, that infamy. It took only twelve men to found it; it will take only one to destroy it." Those who are most vehement in pleas for tolerance are often those most intolerant themselves. Shall we forget that in the early days of America the most vociferous propagandists of tolerance were also those who said it did not apply to "Jews and Papists"?

In vain will we seek to crush anti-Semitism and anti-Christianity and class hatred and bigotry, if our appeals are based only on indifference to truth. Not until we recognize the dignity of human nature as such, created by a loving God and destined for an ineffable union of love with Him, will we find an adequate basis for loving one another. It is charity and not tolerance which must serve as the basis of unity.

There are two philosophies of life: The materialist says: "Man is descended from a monkey. Let us love one another." The Christian, in the words of the Son of God, says: "Love one another as I have loved you." If we came from the beast, then let us act like beasts. If we were made by love, then let us love one another. As the spokes of a wheel are united because they all are united in the hub, so we can be united only in our center who is God.

A good start toward this collaboration of men of good will would be to declare a moratorium on name-calling. Consider the present tendency among those who hate the Catholic Church to call the Church "Fascist"; or the tendency of many good Christians to call all men interested in forward social legislation "Communists"; or the more general tendency to call any one who opposes our pet ideas a "Nazi" and a "friend of Hitler." These "labels" are thrown about on the press and radio as commonly as ignorant boys write dirty words on back fences, and they mean nothing but hate. The Church, as a matter of fact, is no more Fascist than it is Buddhist, but the label "Fascism" is used because the Church is anti-Communist. The legislators, labor organizations and schools which advocate the workers sharing in the profits of capitalism, or a wise government control of monopolies for the common good, are no more "Communist" than they are Japanese, but the term is used solely to provoke hatred by confusing the issue. And because a fellow citizen cannot go into ecstasies about the honesty and integrity of certain foreign governments, but retains a judicial reserve, he is called a "Nazi" and accused of "impeding our war effort." We are indeed at a sorry impasse when a man's patriotism is challenged because he does not love an undemocratic government in a foreign land as much as he loves America.

Love God and love for our neighbor applies to everyone, whomsoever he be, and regardless of his race, class or color. Would that we would lay to heart the words of our President who wrote: "Against enemies who preach the principles of hate and practice them, we shall set our faith in human love and God's care for us, and for all men everywhere."

There are millions who do not share the joys of a Catholic that come from an absolution or a visit to the Real Presence of Christ on the altar, but if any one of us shuts up the bowels of His mercy against a stranger in need, whomsoever he be, the blessing of God cannot be upon him. "And if I should distribute all my goods to feed the poor, and if I should deliver my body to be burned, and have not charity, it profiteth me nothing." Those who glory in the name of Christian forget! "A new commandment I give unto you: That you love one another, as I have loved you, that you also love one another." Shall the Jew forget his Leviticus: "Seek not revenge, nor be mindful of the injury of thy citizen. Thou shalt love thy friend as thyself. I am the Lord." Shall the pagan forget that Aristotle said: "Nothing is more proper to friendship than to share each other's lives."

Unity there must be, not because there is no divine

religious voice in the world, for there is, but because society in abandoning the rule of conscience is on the verge of suicide. It is not a common political way of thinking we must create, for political relativity is the essence of democracy, but the recognition of a common ethos, a universal moral principle which binds all men of all nations of the earth.

There are deeper tensions than those of rival parties, capital and labor, systems of government, namely, the tension in history of the forces of good and evil, the seed of the Woman and the seed of the Beast, the City of God and the City of Satan, the Army of God and the Army of anti-God.

Men of good will: unite! March separately according to the light of your consciences as presently given, but strike together for the moral betterment of the world.

Centuries ago the Star of Bethlehem became the beacon that led the truly Wise Men to the God Whose love became Incarnate and Who preached love God and love your neighbor. On this day millions of stars are out again, shining in the crystal skies of millions of American homes, whence the flower of American manhood ·has gone out to right a world that forgot the meaning of that first star and the Love that lived at the end of its trail.

CHAPTER II

The Pillar of Morality

THE AIR is full of plans, and of pacts and proposals. Every wind that blows through press and air carries patterns for new Leagues, Federal Unions, Spheres of Influence, and Hemisphere Controls, each of which is spread out on the bargain counter of the world, and offered at a price so cheap as to require only a little manipulation of politics and economics—but never change of heart.

There is no quarreling with the necessity of post-war planning, but are we not still suffering from a mental "hangover" from the days of Liberalism and the doctrine of the natural goodness of men? Does not the enthusiastic and fulsome praise we give to every three-hundred-word generalization prove that all we think the world needs is a few structural changes?

Truly, it looks as if our planners think that all we need for peace is to take some of the old rags from international guilt, such as a patch of the primacy of economics, a patch of hatred of *certain* forms of Totalitarianism, a patch of irrelevance of religion and morality here, and patch of the natural goodness of man there, and re-sew them all together in a new way. Thus could we keep ourselves warm in the bed of universal brotherhood while awaiting the sunrise of a brave new world.

What is more important than any plan is to understand what makes one plan right and another plan wrong. Why, for example, a plan to reduce armaments rather than to increase them? Why a plan to grant freedom to certain peoples rather than to enslave them? What we need to know is the basic standard by which all plans can be judged. *Quis custodiet custodes?* Who shall plan the planners? Upon what principle will they operate? Expediency, force or morality?

Thus far we have pleaded for unity among Jews, Protestants and Catholics. This unity, we said, must not be a union of Churches which would do injustice to truth and history, but it must be a unity for social purposes. Now, we ask: what is the one fundamental principle upon which we can unite? Now, we answer it: *The moral law*.

What is the moral law? The moral law is not to be identified with the physical laws of the universe which science studies, for, if science does not put laws into nature as an author, but merely discovers them, as does a proof reader, then who put the laws there? Whenever there is a law, there is a lawmaker, and whenever there is a lawmaker, there is reason.

Neither is the moral law to be identified with the *customs* of primitive people. The primitive people which anthropologists study are not necessarily the original people. But even among these primitive people, the moral law is recognized. Today we find these same people in the Pacific isles scratching their heads, wondering what civilization really means, when they see the so-called superior people butchering one another in mass suicide.

Neither is the moral law to be identified with instinct, because it sometimes contradicts instincts. All the marines at Tarawa had the instinct of self-preservation. What made them suppress that instinct, if there was not a higher moral force impelling them to do so?

What then is moral law? It is a participation or indwelling of the Eternal Reason of God in nature and in man. Everything in the world is governed by law. Falling stones are governed by the law of gravitation, animals by instinct, and man by conscience. God's reason is in each of these things directing them in different ways toward the perfection of their natures. But with man there is a difference. A stone *must* obey its law, but man merely *ought* to obey the law of reason which came from God. A falling star has no freedom; nature is determined. Man is free; therefore he can disobey. Every man, in other words, has a right to make a fool out of himself; and a Calvinist could think of a good adjective. A man is just as free to break the moral law of his conscience as he is free to defy the law of gravitation, but in both instances he hurts himself, because he does what is unreasonable, and it is unreasonable because opposed to the Eternal Reason of God. Immorality therefore is anti-reason.

Now this moral law is not written, except in the sense that St. Paul writes: "It is the law written by the finger of the Creator Himself on the tablets of man's heart."

The moral law, men of good will take for granted; its premises are never mentioned; they are the foundation stones of the house in which we live and to which we but rarely advert. It is not in the front of the mind, but in the back of it; it does not see things, but rather through it we see things; it is the root that is not seen, but without which the fruits of our civilization are impossible.

Almighty God, therefore, has given us an interior Sinai or monitor which speaks to us in His name, tells us before we perform an action whether it is right or wrong, and after we do it, approves, accuses, or excuses. Conscience, therefore, is reason passing judgments on the goodness or malice of our acts.

But how does our reason or conscience decide what is right or wrong? How know whether anything is good or bad? By reason inquiring whether it attains the purpose for which it was made. Everything has a purpose. Reason can discover purposes. A razor has a purpose, namely to shave. But if I pervert that purpose, discoverable by reason, by using the razor to hew a rock, not only do I not hew the rock; I even destroy the razor.

So likewise man's reason tells him he has a purpose: the attainment of truth for his intellect, goodness for his will, and life for his whole being. Whatever contributes to that purpose is good; whatever distorts it is *bad*. As a pencil is good when it writes, for that is its purpose, and as it is bad for opening a can, because that is not its purpose, so man is good when he fulfills the end for which God made him: the attainment of perfect life and truth and love. He is bad when he does not.

Right and wrong therefore are independent of the way people think, because the standard is not public opinion or self-satisfaction, but correspondence with the Eternal Reason of God. You cannot measure cloth except by something that is outside the cloth, and you cannot measure moral ideas and say, for example, that our moral ideas are better than those of the Nazis, except by law outside of both, namely, God.

If morality or decency meant only that we approve, then there could be no right and wrong. Hence, what is all the fighting about? What makes certain notes right on a keyboard and others wrong, if there is nothing but the keys on the piano? What makes one person right and another wrong, if each is a god and a law unto himself? The rightness and wrongness of keys is determined by their correspondence to the score. In like manner, what makes our actions right is the fact that they correspond to the Eternal Reason of God. And this is what we mean by the moral law.

Men of good will accept the moral law. They might not be able to define it, but they speak of it under disguises as "decency," "fair play," "the sporting thing," or that it is wrong to hit a man when he is down, or that stealing, cruelty, rage, treachery, deceit, the shooting of hostages, the deliberate bombing of hospitals and churches, the persecution of Jews, Protestants and Catholics, the systematized starvation of vast populations, *are wrong*; and that the helping of one's neighbor in distress, the feeding of the hungry, the burying of the dead, the love of parents, the love of God, the hatred of evil, the defense of common basic liberties, are right.

Let it not be objected that the moral law is not universal, because the moral ideas of people differ. There are, of course, some instances of degeneration, but the fact that a few people distort the moral law proves nothing against it any more than a mistake in addition proves anything against arithmetic. Furthermore, the moral differences between people are not very big; they certainly are not conventions born of education. Some people drive on the right side of the road and some on the left—this is a convention, but no people believe that desertion from an army is honorable, or that society is an evil, or that the law is opposed to reason, or that a man ought not to do his duty.

The moral law did not originate with Judaism or Christianity. First Judaism and then Christianity brought it to perfection. It originated with man. The pagan Cicero said: "The foundation of law is not opinion, but nature . . . and nothing is ever advantageous if it is not at the same time morally good; and it is only because it is morally good that it is advantageous." When our great and beloved country was founded, it took the moral law for granted; our rights to establish our own government were derived from "the laws of nature and nature's God." In fact, the Declaration of Independence declared that the political dictum of inalienable rights as a gift of God is "self-evident." The Four Freedoms are grounded on the moral law.

Why speak of the moral law? Does not every one accept it? Not any more! That is why we are at war to defend it. There are even some in our midst who do not accept it. One Justice of the Supreme Court, for example, wrote: "The so-called immutable principles must accommodate themselves to facts of life, for facts are stubborn, and must not yield."

This Justice of the Supreme Court should be con-

fronted with one fact: the slaughter of the Jews in
Germany. This is indeed a stubborn fact. Would this
Justice of our Supreme Court say that the moral right
of the Jews to life and freedom should give way to
stubborn facts, and if not, why not? If facts make right,
then the persecution of the Jews is right. Must the immutable principles of right and wrong be changed to
fit the way people live, or must our lives be changed
to fit the immutable principles of right and wrong?
That is the question!

From another well-known American jurist we hear:
"Man must no longer search for God in law." But if
there is no God in law, then there is no morality, and
if no morality, then there is only force—the force of
money, which is Capitalism; the force of steel, which is
Militarism; the force of the masses, which is Nazism,
Fascism and Communism.

Dr. Robert M. Hutchins, summarizing this growing
repudiation of the moral law in American power politics, wrote during the past year: "In law school, I
learned that law was not concerned with reason or justice. Law was what the courts would do. Hitler is what
I would do. There is little to choose between the doc-
trines I learned in an American law school and that
which Hitler proclaims."

Why is there darkness over the earth? For the simple
reason that the moral law has been repudiated in a

wholesale fashion by totalitarian systems and in a retail fashion by some American jurists and intelligentsia— and by the intelligentsia I mean those who have been educated beyond their intelligence. With perfect accuracy did the Holy Father lay his finger on the source of all our woes and wars: "One leading mistake we may single out, and the fountain head, deeply hidden, from which the evils of the modern states derive their origin . . . viz. the setting aside of one universal standard of morality: the Natural Law."

There are only two possible theories of law: law rooted in God and law rooted in force. The whole tradition of western civilization from its beginning in ancient Greece down to the nineteenth century has been based upon the recognition of a common norm of moral law coming from outside man and outside the State, which men have always admitted in principle, even when its application went against them. It has remained for our generation to see the rebirth of another system of law which is grounded either in race, or class or dictatorship, or State or the individual, and which ends only in conflict, for if there is nothing but force, then violence alone can decide what is right. Everything that happens in the future depends on whether the world is to be run by blind irrational forces of power, or to be governed according to certain immutable moral principles with which man can cooperate as a free and rational being. This war is not being fought for political or economic issues; it is being fought to decide whether the moral law of God or the demonic lawlessness of force shall guide the world for the next hundred years.

This basic moral law of reason, which is a participation of each of us in the Eternal Reason of God, is the one principle upon which all can unite. It makes no difference if one be a Jew, a Protestant or a Catholic, a Hottentot, a Mohammedan, Hindu, German or Japanese. For as Gladstone wrote in the last century: "The moral law is coeval with mankind and dictated by God Himself, and is of course superior in obligation to any other. It is binding all over the globe in all countries and at all times; no human laws are of any validity, if contrary to this."

Why does not the moral law play a more important role in our lives today? Because we have so concentrated on the wickedness of our military enemies, that we have excused ourselves from asking if we ourselves obey the moral law. We lay the whole burden for the mess of the world on Hitler, and no one doubts that Hitler has contributed generously. But if Hitler died tomorrow, would peace and virtue automatically follow? Because disorder reigns we feel some one must be blamed. We blame Hitler. Hitler blames the Jews and the Bolsheviks; the pinks blame the Catholics, and on and on it goes. Hitler thus becomes the scapegoat who takes away the sins of the rest of the world.

Evil is thus always put outside ourselves. As a result, everywhere there is Hate! Hate! Hate! Some well-known writers in this country have suggested extermi-nating all Germans. Others have asked that Hitler be put in a cage and paraded through the streets so on-lookers could hiss at him! No wonder there is anti-Semitism! No wonder there is anti-Christianity! No wonder there is bigotry!

The war has taught us to despise and, in teaching us to despise, has given us a moral superiority which blinds us to our infractions of the moral law; to juvenile de-linquency, increased divorces, selfishness among capi-talists, selfishness among certain labor leaders and the rejection of the moral law by so many jurists in high places. Our hate has turned this war into a negative, not a positive war, a war in which we know what we are fighting against, but not a war in which we know what we are fighting for! Only Germany and Japan have a positive goal, a definite purpose—and it is as wicked and as evil as hell. Russia, too, knows what it wants—but that is another matter.

But for too many this war has only a *negative* mean-ing: Ask your fellow citizen what it is about and he will tell you, "To kill with Hitler and Tojo." If he uses a slogan such as "liberty" he will define it negatively in terms of freedom *from* these two dictators!

Do we think that peace will come because we put Hitler in a cage? Did peace come from exiling the Kaiser to a woodpile? Shall it be said of us that we are united only because we have a common hate? Do we think that victory in arms alone will save civilization? Once we defeat those who would destroy freedom by force, do we automatically defeat those who would use freedom to destroy freedom?

Is not this war rather to preserve the moral law of God against the powers of darkness that challenge it? If that be so, why do we not humble ourselves before God? How many of us can go to the corpse of this tragic world and lay our hand upon its cold flesh and say: "I am innocent"? We all stand in need of God's mercy and pardon, and particularly our own country because to it has been given the high mission and vocation of defending man and therefore the rights of God.

America is not God! England is not God! Russia is not God! We are not the Creators of law; we are only its trustees. We are not the womb of freedom; we are the feeble instruments God uses to break chains that men may be free on the outside as they are already free on the inside. We are not the Saviours of the world; we too stand in need of salvation. May we be defenders, at home and in the world, of this moral law! May God in His Mercy preserve us, bless us and lead us to victory! It is not God that needs America. It is America that needs God!

CHAPTER III

The Pillar of Property

THE BASIC moral principle in the economic order is: *The right to property is personal; the use of property is common.* Of the two: personal rights and common use —*use* is more fundamental than *right*, because God created the universe for all men, and not for the particular exploitation of any one group or class. Hence, if a man were starving, and had exhausted all other legitimate means of acquiring food, he might seize from his neighbor that which was necessary for his life. In this particular instance, the use is prior to the right. Among other reasons what justifies the personal *right* to property is that man will do most to develop it, administer it, when he has some control over it. No citizen picks up papers in the park. The park belongs to every one. But we do pick up papers in our own back yard.

Furthermore, *private property is the economic guarantee of human freedom. Economic* guarantee, for the *spiritual* guarantee of freedom is the fact that each man has a soul he can call his own. But there must be some *external* sign of that inner freedom, *i.e.,* something he can call his own on the *outside,* because he calls his soul his own on the inside. Freedom means responsibility for one's acts, but how can this interior mastery of one's acts be better guaranteed than by the ownership of something external over which he can exercise control?

Just as an artist is most free to express his spiritual ideas when he owns the canvas, the brush, and the paints, so man knows he is responsible when he exercises responsibility. Because the owner of shares of stock admits no responsibility to his ownership, he ignores the rights of workers, and because the worker *has* no responsibility, he may stop work even when the nation needs it. Hence private property is the external guarantee of human freedom. That is why slaves were deemed not to be free, because they had no property. *They were property*. Morality says: Because *I am*, I may *have*: to *have* is the legitimate extension of my *being*. Property and freedom are one and the same problem.

This principle of personal right and social use avoids both the one extreme error of Liberalism and Capitalism which makes the right to property absolute, and the extreme error of Communism which denies personal rights altogether by overstressing common use. We have become so accustomed to emphasizing property rights, that we completely ignore the fact that God made this world for all men. We forget that around each person there are various circles or zones, some very close to personality, others very distant. In the first zone are my rights to things which are *absolutely necessary*, food, clothing, habitation, and all the normal necessities of life, sufficient for self and family. In a second outer zone are things that are *relatively necessary* because of a peculiar position or state of life, or because one uses these superfluities for the good of others. In a still outer zone are things that are not necessary at all—luxuries, such as a yacht.

The repudiation of moral principles today has confused these zones or blurred them all into one, so that one uses the term "my" to cover them all without any distinction. For example, the modern man will speak of "my food," "my house," "my car," "my servant," "my gallery," "my stamp collection," "my private golf course," "My Paris residence," even "my God" with exactly the same stress on "my" as if the right to the outer zones was equal to the right of the inner zones, and as if the possessive pronoun was no different when I say "my bread" and "my bonds."

The moral law, on the contrary, affirms that the right to property varies in direct ratio to how close or how far away these zones of ownership are to personality. The nearer things are to our inner responsibility, the stronger the right to ownership; the nearer the "I," the stronger the "have," as the nearer we get to the fire, the greater the heat. That is why, incidentally, the right of a head of a corporation to his second million does not equal the right of a worker to share in the wealth which he has helped to create. The right to property, therefore, is not absolute and invariable.

The right to property and the use of property are therefore not bounded by the same limits. For example, a man may have a just right to the wine in his cellar. He may have acquired title to it honestly through his own labor. But he may not *use* that wine as he pleases. He may not call in his neighbor's children and put them all in a state of "amiable incandescence." And if he does, he violates the commandment against temperance and not the commandment about property rights. We have rights to things, but may not use them as we please.

Property has a double aspect: individual and social. The right is personal; the use is social. Hence, in a well-ordered society the two are inseparable, for whenever there is a right there is a responsibility. For example, I may have the right to a cow, but if I allow my cow to graze in your victory garden, I must remunerate you. And when the cow dies, I must bury it. My *right* to my cow is bound up with responsibility, or my *use* of the cow.

These principles are clear in relation to cows, houses, farms, pianos and pigeons. But when one enters the field of modern industry, the application of the principles of right and responsibility is not so easy. This is because modern Capitalism has divorced *right* and *use*, or responsibility. Great industries are generally not owned by one man, but by millions. No one individual owns over four per cent of the Bell Telephone Company. The right is diffused through stocks. But notice the difference between the ownership of a cow and the ownership of stock. Because I have a right to my cow, I am clearly responsible for the way I use it. But how many who own stocks feel any responsibility? How many who are stockholders in corporations are concerned as to whether the workers receive a living wage, or whether their rights of collective bargaining are recognized, or whether their hours are too long? The fact is that stockholders are concerned only with their *rights* to property, not with their *responsibilities* or use of property. There are instances of individuals who owned ten shares in a railroad, walking into a directors' meeting and insisting upon exercising some responsibility toward its operation, but the incidents were written up as humor in the newspaper.

The fact is that under finance-Capitalism there has been a divorce of right from responsibility, or use. Generally those who own the stocks do not manage or work or exercise any responsibility. And those who manage or exercise responsibility do not own. As family life has broken down because of the divorce of husband and wife, so the economic life has broken down because of the divorce of capital from responsibility and the divorce of labor from its tools and their fruits. The result is, we have capitalists who do not labor, and labor leaders who are capitalists, in the sense that they do not labor.

Thus, the two elements of private property which are clearly united in the ownership of a cow—responsibility and use—are divorced in the ownership of capitalistic enterprises. The owner of the cow could claim *all* profits from the cow, because he owned the cow and was responsible for it. But the owner of stocks claims all the profits because he *owns* the stock, though he disowns responsibility. He has surrendered *half* of his title to profits, namely, responsibility, but lays claim to *all* the profits.

This does not mean that the moral principle concerning private property is wrong; it only means that the system is wrong. Now, how make it right? By granting to those who manage, use, work in, and are responsible for the production of profits some *share* in the social wealth which they have helped to create. If a farmer keeps his right to the cow, but surrenders its responsibility and care and use to a hired man, he at least ought to give that hired hand a glass of the milk.

"Property," we read in the Papal Encyclical, *Quadragesimo Anno,* "that is 'capital,' has undoubtedly long been able to appropriate too much to itself. Whatever was produced, whatever returns accrued, capital claimed for itself, hardly leaving enough to restore and renew the worker's strength.". . ."This gave rise to the equally fictitious moral principle, that all products and profits, save only enough to repair and renew capital, belong by very right to the worker."

The moral law suggests that one class is forbidden to exclude the other from sharing in the benefits. Hence, the stockholding class violates this law when it thinks that it ought to get everything and the worker nothing. So does the non-owning working class when, angered deeply at outraged justice, it demands for itself everything as if produced by its own hands alone, and attacks and seeks to abolish, therefore, all property and returns or incomes.

"Therefore, with all our strength and effort we must strive that at least in the future the abundant fruits of production will accrue equitably to those who are rich and will be distributed in ample sufficiency among the workers—not that these may become remiss in work, for man is born to labor as the bird to fly—but that they may increase their property by thrift. . . . We consider it more advisable, however, in the present condition of human society that, so far as is possible, the work-contract be somewhat modified by a partnership-contract as is already being done in various ways and with no small advantage to the workers and owners. Work-

ers and other employees thus become sharers in ownership or management or participate in some fashion in
the profits received."

The moral law suggests a *partnership contract* between capital and labor to such an extent that the
worker share in some way in the ownership, management, or profits of industry.

This partnership may involve three things:

(1) The right of employees to participate in the
management of the industry by having one or more of
their members represent them on the Board of Directors.

(2) The right of employees to share in the *ownership*
of industry, through special labor shares which ought
not to be subject to market fluctuation of capital shares,
and which should give them the right to vote on the
distribution of dividends, even though it means chang-
ing the corporate structure.

(3) The right of employees to share in the *profits* of
industry over and above a just wage, since they did
more to create those profits than the money-lender with
his stock certificate. The profits to be distributed must
not be those profits left after a fat dividend has been
declared to stockholders. They should be those over
and above an amount agreed upon by Capital and
Labor as a minimum, and not those set arbitrarily by
Capital alone. For example, in the Gospels, the wage

principle of the laborers in the vineyard was not merely compensation for the work done, because all received the same wage, even those who worked only for an hour. There are therefore other factors governing just remuneration than wages for work done.

The advantages of this co-partnership are many: if Capital wants Labor to become interested in its work, it ought to give Labor some capital to defend. A man is willing to sit down on some one else's tools, but he is not willing to sit down on his own. As regards labor, co-partnership will restore the vocation of work; it will transform a factory from a place where men find fault to a place where they find some joy. Having regained some self-respect, they will try to do as much as possible instead of trying to do as little as possible. Labor will feel that it is then working for itself as well as for the employer, and it will be to its advantage to increase output and reduce waste.

Finally, as far as both Capital and Labor are concerned, it will mean they will cease seeing how much each can get out of the other but how much both can get out of common enterprise, thus creating a true industrial democracy. We will never have complete democracy in this country until we extend its blessings· from politics to economics.

Thus, co-partnership has been opposed by Capital and Labor, and too often for selfish reasons. Capital refused to allow workers to share in the management of business and in the profits. And now it finds that management and profits are to a great extent being taken over by the government, with the result that neither Capital nor Labor get the profits.

Labor leaders too have often been shortsighted. They were against sharing this partnership, because they feared that the workers might become more attached to the employer than to them if they received the profits. It was a question of whether they should have dues or the worker profits, and the fear of alienation of affection drove them to make increasing demands for higher wages instead of co-partnership. If economics is to be reduced to a question of courtship, let the best man win.

Outside the wider diffusion of private property here suggested there are three solutions possible:

One is to keep the right to property in the hands of monopolistic Capitalism, cartels and corporations, and thus create a servile State, even while satisfying the unions' demands every twelve months.

Another solution is Communism and Socialism which would remedy individual selfishness by collective selfishness, i.e., by putting all the property in the hands of the State, and substituting for monopoly by Capitalism a monopoly by Party. Communism is thus State Capitalism; it hates Capitalism because it wants to be capitalistic itself. Every Communist is a Capitalist without any cash in his pockets; he is an involuntary Capitalist. And as for the worker, there is little to choose between living at the sufferance of a Capitalist or living at the sufferance of a Party leader, for in either case, so long as he lives *by the will* of another he is not free.

A third solution is Bureaucracy, or Capitalistic Fascism, which normally, instead of diffusing profits by giving some of it to the workers, collects profits in the form of taxes from industry, passes it through a thousand government offices, and then gives the residue as dole.

The worker who depends entirely and immediately upon the State for his security, as is the tendency today, and not upon private ownership, eases his condition for a moment. But ultimately bureaucracy by a slow evolution ends in the abduction of personal dignity. Either we must diffuse ownership of private property or we will destroy *freedom*, for the abolition of private property is the beginning of slavery. Wherever property is, there is power. Put it into the hands of Monopolistic Capitalism and it will dictate how to vote; put it in the hands of the State, and the State will dictate the vote, for as Alfred E. Smith once said: "No one wants to kill Santa Claus."

This moral solution of the economic problem is hardly ever discussed. It has been said that the American people must choose between Individualism and Collectivism: between a system in which the individual manages everything without government interference, and Collectivism, in which the State manages everything without individual interference.

No! There is a golden mean in the economic problem: one in which the property rights are diffused through co-partnership, instead of being concentrated either in the hands of Capitalists or in the hands of the State. The State must *guarantee* the social security of its citizens, but it must not *supply* that security. Freedom from want must not be purchased by freedom from freedom, in which a Bureaucratic State becomes the world's caterer. There is a world of difference between re-distribution of income through the taxation chiefly of wage earners, as the Beveridge Plan suggests, and the re-distribution of created wealth at the source, namely, *production*. There is an alternative to the reign of money in society, which is Capitalism, and the reign of the State which is Socialism; between a government of laws and a government of bureaucratic management; between a government in which the State is a policeman, and a government in which the State is a nurse; between *laissez faire* and dictatorship; between a system in which a few Capitalists get all the eggs and the workers the shells, and a system in which the Socialistic State gets all the eggs and makes an omelet; and that alternation is, a system in which the hens are shared.

When you get down to rock bottom, what objection is there to the suggestion of the decentralization of property so that Capitalism and Labor are made co-partners in industry? Basically, there is only one: selfishness. So long as there is no spiritual force to harness the wild acquisitive instincts, at what point will the Capitalist say: "Please, no more profits. I have already made 8 per cent on my money." As a matter of fact, one capitalist said: "If this war goes on two more years, I could make a million."

At what point will Labor say: "Desist. Our wages are high enough! Our hours are short enough!" One of the largest labor journals wrote one week: "Let us prove to the boys at the front, that we can work harder and produce more for them." Three days later 125,000 of them were on strike for higher wages!

Given the unrestrained lust for money on the part of Capitalism and Labor, there will be no stopping until both die of their own too much. Socialism is no answer to the problem, simply because Socialism is not social. Any State which concentrates property in its hands is the enemy of the people, and any theory which attempts to correct the irresponsibility of either Capitalism or Labor by making them both irresponsible, has killed the free personality of man as much as an apple dumpling destroys the individuality of an apple. To cure this unbounded selfishness, the State has had to interfere with Capitalism, to preserve some semblance of the common good, and it will soon have to interfere with Labor for the same reason. So long as Capitalism and Labor regard the other as so much carrion upon which as vultures they may devour their fill, the common good of a free and decent America will be only a cemetery wherein ghouls may feed on buried treasure.

This is basic: the selfish, acquisitive spirit of Capital and Labor must be crushed if we are ever to have economic peace and security.

There are two ways to kill it. Neither of these methods lies in the economic order; one is in the political, the other in the spiritual. The first kills selfishness from the outside; the other from the inside. The first is the way of the Nazi, Fascist, and Communist which destroys freedom. It works for a time. For example, Germany was at the top of the exporting countries of the world; Fascism even had the trains running on time; and Communism had no more unemployment than Sing Sing—and for the same reason. But in killing selfishness the Socialistic way, these systems killed free enterprise and free men.

There is one other way open to us, and that is to crush selfishness from the inside by a spiritual rebirth, for not until we begin living for the moral law of God will we ever live for one another.

Something radical must be done! We cannot go on

as we have. It is positively a disgrace for any country to have plenty of work and plenty of money only when it is engaged in the dirty business of war. Shall our selfish interests be killed only while we are killing? Shall we work as a united nation for the good of all only when Mars sits on our altars? This much is certain: Any nation that can provide work in war can provide work in peace. Work for all, and security for all.

To suggest that the solution of our economic problem is not in the economic order, but in the moral, is to bring down upon one's offending head the charge: the suggestion is impractical. Certainly it is impractical! That is why it will work. When things are half out of order any tinker or bureaucratic planner can fix them, but when the world is in a mess, it takes more than a practical solution.

It is just as impracticable as saying: "Seek ye first the kingdom of God and his justice; and all these things shall be added unto you."

Our choice is not between individualism and collectivism; it is between a mechanistic socialistic collectivism and a moral spiritual collectivism.

Capitalists will not like this suggestion of co-partnership because it means reduced profits. Labor leaders will not like it because it will mean less dues, but men of good will will like it because it will create a new America where no man will claim a right without acknowledging a duty. An America where Capital will do some labor, and Labor will have some capital; where the right to property will be personal and where the use of property will be common; where no one will recognize he is free until all are free; and where none can be free until he submits to that Truth of God which makes all men free, and in making all men free, makes them Americans!

CHAPTER IV

The Pillar of Personality

THE BASIC moral principle of the political order is: *The State exists for the person; not the person for the State.*

Democracy is founded on this moral principle. Totalitarianism in all its forms, on the contrary, believes the person exists for the State.

Why in the United States does the State exist for the person?

Because the person is prior *in origin* to the State, i.e., he existed before the State. God made man according to His image and likeness; and man made the State according to his image and likeness. The government therefore derives its just powers from the consent of the governed, and the governed get theirs from God.

The State exists for the person because the person is nobler *in nature* than the State; the person has an eternal destiny, whereas the State has only a temporal destiny. The State is not a distinct entity from the persons who comprise it. A citizen is a person with an eternal destiny who works out his salvation in time, while living in a State.

The State exists for the person because the person,

having an immortal soul, is the subject of rights. Centipedes have no rights, nor have cabbages, and they have no rights because they have no souls.

This moral truth of the supremacy of the person is enshrined in our Constitution and in our American traditions.

Our Declaration of Independence declares, "It is a self-evident principle that *the Creator* has endowed man with certain inalienable rights, among which are the right to life, liberty and the pursuit of happiness." To our Founding Fathers it was clear to every one that these rights and freedom flowed from a Divinely Created personality. To safeguard further this self-evident principle the Ninth Amendment to the Constitution stated that it must not be assumed that the people have no rights other than those given to them by the Constitution. In other words, since rights and liberties were not State-given, but God-given, they existed before any State. The only reason a government was instituted was, in the language of the Declaration of Independence, "to secure those rights," i.e., to protect and safeguard rights already existing in virtue of the value of the human person created by God.

In establishing our government on the principle that the State exists for the person, our political forebears were merely reiterating the great Christian tradition that the supreme value on this earth is the human person, because God made him, because Christ died for his sins, and the Holy Spirit sanctified him. Not upon any psychological or anthropological or biological theories concerning man was this democratic doctrine grounded, but upon the Christian tradition that a single man is precious because he has an immortal soul. What, therefore, our ancestors in the Declaration of Independence called "self-evident" was in reality a matter of faith and tradition. No chemical analysis or biological proddings, or psychological soundings, will show that the slaves, the refugees, the Jews, the so-called "Papists," John Jones and Baron Rothschild, Mary Smith and Queen Elizabeth were "all created free and equal" and all entitled to "life, liberty and the pursuit of happiness." This idea comes from theology and not from anthropology. It comes from the natural law and faith, not from human law and sentimentalism.

It was part and parcel of a large synthesis: as God is in the universe, but transcendent and superior to it; as the Kingdom of God is in the world, but not of it; as the soul is in the body but not immersed and identical with it, so the human person is in the State but does not exist solely for the State. What was latent in the minds of our Founding Fathers was explicitly stated five centuries before by St. Thomas in a phrase that needs to be remembered by every statesman today: "Man is not subordinated to the body politic to the whole extent of all he is and all that he has. For a man's whole being and powers and possessions must be referred to God."

Our Constitution puts politics under theology, democracy under God. But today, politics denies its divine foundation. Politics is today the supreme and absolute science. We once lived in the age of the Theological Man; then came the age of the Economic Man; now we are in the age of Political Man. The Theological Man lived for God; the Economic Man lived for profit; the Political Man lives for the State.

The Theological Man believed he came from God into this earth as a kind of novitiate, and that some day he would go back to God to render an account of his stewardship. There are still theological creatures in the world, but there are not enough of them to give a tone and temper to the society in which we live. They are the exception; once they were the rule

About one hundred years ago the Economic Man came into being. He was not concerned with saving his soul, but with making money. For if this life is all, why not get all we can out of it? He insisted that freedom be understood as the absence of law and restraint, in order that he could accumulate as much wealth as he wished.

Into that age of the Economic Man, there came Karl Marx, the founder of Communism, and also the spiritual father of the Political Man. He had one good thought, and one very bad one. His good idea was that, if men were allowed freedom to make as much money as they pleased, we should soon reach a condition where wealth would be concentrated in the hands of the few, while the masses would become impoverished. His bad idea was the plan to prevent this: namely, put all property into the hands of the State, thus making the State supply the needs of the citizens.

Now once you put property into the hands of the State you concentrate power, for property is power. And once power is in the hands of the State, men want to be where that power is in order that they might distribute it. Thus was begotten the Political Man who as the new Capitalist seeks the new wealth, which is not money but privilege.

What economics was to the days of Liberalism, politics is to the Modern Man. So important has politics become, that now men judge religion by its attitude toward politics, rather than politics by its attitude toward religion. It is like judging health by the kind of a plate from which one eats.

How did politics become so important? Through a loss of the moral law. In the days when Christianity was the soul of civilization, when all men recognized they had a common end, both eternal and temporal, politics and economics held a secondary place. No one system of politics was absolutely right; they were all means to an end, purely relative in character, and varied with the background, and traditions and nature of a given society. This is why St. Thomas, in discussing three possible forms of politics, is not absolutely certain which he preferred. The Church has always taught that one form of government is not absolutely better than any other form of government, so long as the person is recognized as superior to the State.

But today, when men abandon a common philosophy of life, i.e., when they disagree about ends, viz., why we are living, where we are going, whether God exists, whether the moral law should be obeyed, they begin to concentrate their attention upon *means*, and principally upon systems of politics. Politics thus becomes an absolute. Once men agreed that to enjoy shooting, men should have a common target—the kind of arrows they used being of little importance. Today, they disagree about the target and insist every one should use the same arrow. Once when men sat down at table, they were agreed on the necessity of eating; now they disagree on eating, and quarrel about the knives and forks. When men agreed on the purpose of life, they admitted political relativities. But now they differ on the purpose of life, they make politics a theology and erect the means of life, about which there should be legitimate disagreement, into an end of life about which no man may disagree.

That is why in all the totalitarian countries, e.g., Russia, Germany, and Italy up until the political demise, there is only *one party*. Every one must think alike, and where every one thinks alike, there is no thinking.

The result is that politics enjoys the same status that theology enjoyed in a Christian society, and appropriates even the same emotions which once surrounded religion. The heretics today are enemies of a party, not enemies of God's Truth. Fascism, Nazism and Communism have their inquisitorial sanctions which makes the religious persecutions of the past pale into insignificance. The modern man would only smile if you told him his attitude was not Christian, but he would knock you down if you told him he was a Fascist.

That word "Fascism" is never defined. It often means every one who is anti-Communistic; sometimes it means one who believes in God, or authority, or religion. As a matter of fact, we do not know what Fascism is; it is the subjection of the person to the State, as Nazism is the subjection of the person to the race, and as Communism is the subjection of the person to the class. But that is too clear cut to satisfy the muddle-minded. They want to keep it undefined, so as to beat down with a sneer any one who refuses to accept their political outlook. Every one is so touchy about politics. To say a word against Russia today would be regarded by many as more serious than to blaspheme the Holy Spirit of God. In fact, if one says it is cold in

Moscow, he is called a Fascist. Well! It is cold in Russia. All the intolerance which once surrounded Absolute Truth and the multiplication table is now bestowed to the relativity of politics. The relative of a Christian society thus becomes the absolute of a pagan society.

One could go through history and find a dozen historical instances to prove that, as men lose their belief in God, the State becomes an Absolute. Men must have a god, and if it will not be the God of hearts, it will be the State god. About the time of the birth of Christ, religion had reached its lowest ebb in Rome and it was the moment when the State became Absolute and the Caesars deified. Vergil spoke of Caesar Augustus as of "Divine Origin"; Pompey called himself "god"; Cicero said, "Augustus came from heaven"; Herod paraded before the people in silvered costume, letting his subjects burn incense before him with the flattery: "It is the voice of god, and not the voice of man."

Fifteen centuries later when religion ceased to be a unifying power of men, the State began to assert itself, and the Divine Right of Kings became the secular substitute of the Divine Right of the Vicar of the King of Kings. Finally, in our day, Stalin has permitted himself to be called "Creator of World Order," while Hitler has declared himself greater than Christ.

What are the effects of the absoluteness of politics?—

The most general effect is the dehumanization of man. Once man became loosened from his divine moorings, he became "autonomous," or an independent god. But no State could survive if every man was a god and a law unto himself, any more than a machine would work if every little wheel in it turned according to its own selfish ends.

To change the figure men became as so many independent atoms without reference to any other universe than themselves. It was natural, therefore, for some powerful dictator to arise and say, "Well, we must now organize you into a unity." This unity became the collectivity of the race which was Nazism, of the State which was Fascism, and of the class which was Communism. From that point on, freedom and rights took on a new meaning. Freedom was no longer in man; it was in the race, the nation, the class. A man was free only when he thought, acted and willed as the Dictator bade. Rights, in like manner, were no longer in man, for if God did not give him rights, how could he have rights? Rights were only in the totality or the herd; man was *given* rights; but he possessed none.

In democracies, the dehumanization of man has taken an academic or quasi-scientific background. The whole tendency of our thinking for the last seventy years has been to destroy man's dignity by identifying him with nature, i.e., with the stones and the beasts.

Evolution, for example, made him one with the animal in his *origin*; Behaviorism identified him with the animal in his *actions*, and his *nature*; Freudianism identified him with the animal in his *mental processes*; Pragmatism identified him with the animal in his *goals* and *purposes*. What follows? If man is one with nature, then why should he not be treated as nature, i.e., as a *thing*, or a *means* to an *end*. Human rights and freedom lost their outside purchase in God, where the Declaration of Independence put them. In fact all rights and liberties disappeared, for nature has no rights. The result is that a new system of law, or political theory, has arisen which makes law merely a positive fact like a poker or a broom.

Democracy With God	*Democracy Without God*
Rights come to us from God.	Our rights come to us from the State.
Because rights are God-given they are inalienable.	Since the State gives rights, the State can take them away.
Law is the reflection of the Eternal Reason of God and therefore any law which contradicts it is unjust.	Man is the creator of law, and whatever the courts decide is just.
All men are equal because all are made to the image of God, and all are destined for the same end.	All men are equal, because all men, since they are creators of their own law, are all gods.

If the moral basis of politics is rejected, the nation falls, for unless the electorate votes from an informed conscience rather than on the basis of propaganda, a democracy can vote itself right out of a democracy— as Germany did.

A triple obligation is incumbent upon us:

(1) Preserve the moral law in domestic politics. One of the grave dangers to the world is Fascism, either black, brown or red. Here I speak of Red Fascism or Communism, because the black and brown Fascism arose only in reaction to the Red. In this connection, it might be well to realize that the so-called "dissolution" of the Third International was only a change of coat, not a change of heart. Communism today is dressing up. It tells us that it will no longer function as a political party in the United States. And why? Because it has discovered that by supporting either one or the other of the two major political parties, as circumstances demand, it can place more Communists in key positions of government than if it depended on the ballot and the common sense of the American people.

Communist agents will no longer talk revolution against our government; rather they will seek to make it conform itself to the foreign policy of Communism. America can be destroyed in one of two ways: by a revolt against it, or by selling its soul. Communism now chooses to corrupt its soul. From now on the Communist agent is no longer a domestic revolutionist; he is a foreign diplomat. He is no longer a Bolshevik; he is an educator. America is the sea in which he fishes; the bait is in "international unity" and the poor fish who bite best are the pinks and the intellectuals. Please God, not too many have scales on their backs!

(2) Keep America on the single standard, by conforming to the moral law of God. Once human law loses its objective standard, it becomes absurd to speak of any policy or law as being right or wrong. Right becomes "legality," or whatever happens is right. The result would be a double standard of morality. We must not have one code for certain nations, and another code for other nations. It would be wrong when one country absorbs another into itself to say: "Go to war." But when a third country absorbs still another into itself to say: "It will make for a world peace." It would be wrong, when one form of Totalitarianism extinguishes all other parties and allows no freedom of press, to call it "Fascism," and when another country does exactly the same thing to call it "Democracy." It would be wrong, when one country breaks a treaty with another to defend its selfish interests, to call it "international banditry," and when another country does it to call it "self-defense." It would be wrong to have one standard for soldiers and another for civilians in defense plants, calling it a "crime" for the soldier to desert his post of

duty and calling it "progress" when a defense worker deserts his duty. There must be no choosing between barbarities. Right is right if nobody is right, and wrong is wrong if everybody is wrong.

(3) Love America as a duty. Patriotism is a form of piety. And there are three principle forms of piety: love of God, love of neighbor, and love of country. All three are grounded in justice.

It is an historical fact that a country begins to decline at that moment when its citizens begin to love a foreign power more than its own. This happens the very moment justice and morality cease to be the root of patriotism. It happened, for example, when Frederick the Great refused to learn German and became so enamored of the godlessness of France that he loved it more than decent traditions of his own land. The spiritual zero of morality was reached when Frederick invited Voltaire to Germany to absorb some of his atheistic irresponsibility. When these two individuals looked into one another's empty souls, they made a sneer that was as eternal as the smile of a skull. What Frederick did to the moral heritage of his people, we must not do with ours.

In a time of crisis, the difference between those who believe in and live by the moral law, and those who do not, becomes intensified. The less moral we are, the less Christian, the less God-fearing, the less we protest against the disruption of family life by divorces and the like, the more we will be accepted by this world, as Our Lord was accepted on Palm Sunday when it was thought that His ideas coincided with those of the mob. But the more Christian we become, the more God-fearing we are, the more we insist on morality in education, family life and politics, the more we will be regarded with suspicion and with hate. Our very existence will be regarded as a danger. We need do nothing to bring a reaction against us, any more than the early Christians of Rome, who were good citizens, were guilty of any other crime than that of refusing to call Nero "Fuehrer" or god.

We will be hated because our moral code is a reproach to the world. The word of Our Lord will be verified: "If you had been of the world, the world would love its own: but because you are not of the world, but I have chosen you out of the world, therefore the world hateth you."

So strong is this spirit growing in the world today, that one can predict with infallible accuracy which of two contending groups in any State in Europe will be favored by most of those journalists, commentators and publicists who are making world opinion; it will invariably be that party, that group, that underground whose background is irreligious, or atheistic or even anti-Christian.

As the world grows into an ideological uniformity in which all men are supposed to think alike, the believer in the moral law and particularly the Church will come in increasing conflict with it, and for no other reason than that they assert and believe in God and the moral law! The great scene in the courtroom of the Roman Governor may be repeated, when Pilate said to Our Lord: "Knowest thou not that I have power to crucify thee, and I have the power to release thee?" To him the Saviour answered: "Thou shouldst not have any power against me, unless it were given thee from above."

This is at the heart of the present world conflict— that of State-given rights and of God-given rights. Because that conflict was destined to come to the surface, it was kept in the Creed and we still repeat it daily. In the truest sense of the word, the Church and men of good will are now "suffering under Pontius Pilate."

One thing we must never do is to purchase a transitory freedom by the sacrifice of God's truth! If the choice is to stultify ourselves by sacrificing our moral being for a false peace, or to endure persecution, let us in God's name choose the ennoblement of a persecution. "And fear ye not them that kill the body and are not able to kill the soul: but rather fear him that can destroy both soul and body in hell."

That brings us back to the beginning. What is an American? An American is one who believes that his

rights and liberties come to him from God, and that
they are therefore inalienable, and that no State on the
face of God's earth can take them away. On April 30,
1777, George Washington, fearful that some of his men
were more loyal to foreign powers than to their own
country, posted up an order that was to be obeyed absolutely at night. And now as men forget God and darkness settles over the earth we needs must repost that
order of Washington. "Put none but Americans on
guard tonight." How true! It is night! Put none but
Americans on guard!

CHAPTER V

The Pillar of the Family

THE BASIC moral principle of Domestic Society is: *The family is the natural unit of society and the right of education belongs primarily to the parents, not to the State.*

The family in the *natural order* is the only Divine Institution in the world. God did not found the American Chamber of Commerce, the C.I.O., the National League, or the U.S.S.R., but in making man and woman, who find the natural complement in one another, and whose children are the incarnation of their mutual love, God did found the family.

As the family is the divinely-organized society of the natural order, so the Church is the divinely-organized society of the supernatural order. Since grace is built upon nature, the Church cannot destroy the natural rights of society. The family, therefore, as a society, precedes both the State and the Church.

Since the family is the natural unit of society and precedes both the State and the Church in nature and in time, it follows that the parents, and not the State, have the primary and normal right of education. The family holds directly from the Creator the inalienable right to educate. This right is inviolable by any power on earth, as is evident from the fact that the education of the children is the concern of the parents long before it is the concern of any one else. The State exists for the family, the family does not exist for the State.

The parents may, if they wish, delegate the exercise of this right to the State, but even then the primary responsibility for the education of the child remains with the parent, not with the teacher. The teacher only *supplements*, but never *supplants* either the right or duty of parents. The function of the State, when it receives this delegation, is merely to protect and foster but never to absorb either the individual or the family, or to substitute itself for them.

The teacher always acts in the name of the parents, not in the name of the State; though the State, to safeguard its citizenship, may guarantee the efficiency of the teachers. A teacher receives his mission from humanity, not from the government. Whatever authority he exercises over the children to teach, control, and discipline them comes from God, through the parents, and not from the State, except insofar as the State acts on behalf of the parents. To make the teacher the representative of the State, as in Nazi Germany, is to make him the guardian of a party, its fleeting policies, its ideologies, its theories, and thus an enemy of culture, of tradition, and of humanity.

This basic principle of domestic society, that the primary and normal right of education belongs to the parents and not to the State, is a conclusion of the moral law. It is not Catholic Doctrine exclusively, though it has wrongly become identified as Catholic teaching. As a matter of fact it is part of the legal tradition of the United States enthroned in both the Fourteenth Amendment and the decisions of the Supreme Court.

For example, the Supreme Court of the United States handed down this decision: "The fundamental theory of liberty upon which all governments in the Union repose, excludes any general power of the State to standardize its children by forcing them to accept instruction from public teachers only. The child is not the mere creature of the State: those who nurture him and direct his destiny have the right, coupled with high duty, to recognize and prepare him for additional obligations."

This principle is denied by all totalitarian ideologies which affirm that the total man, body and soul, belongs to the State. It is also denied by some of those intelligentsia and so-called "expert" educators at home. In a survey made by Dr. A. P. Raup of 2000 students seeking teaching certificates in 70 institutions, it was discovered that 50 per cent of them had been indoctrinated by naturalist teachers who denied both the moral law and the existence of any rights except State-given rights, and whose basic assumption was that man is an animal.

Too many parents today shift their responsibility to the school and assume that by doing so they have fulfilled their parental obligations. Have they forgotten that the education of their children is their concern seven years before it is the concern of the school? A rough calculation will show too that, when schooling starts, the child still spends about 85 per cent of his time at home. The child has been given by God to the parents as so much putty in their hands; and how the little ones will be moulded and formed is the primary responsibility of the home. There is such a thing in the Providence of God as "mother-craft" and "father-craft," but there never was a time when these noble professions were in such danger of being lost. Sending a child to school no more acquits the parents of responsibility than sending a child to a swimming pool acquits the parents of responsibility for that child's cleanliness.

What has complicated and intensified parental irresponsibility is the fact that most schools today assume that education consists only of the *imparting of knowledge*. This is an egregious error, because knowledge is only a part of education. The whole man must be educated, and this means the will must be trained as well as the intellect. More important than knowledge is the formation of character, the right ordering of conscience, and the formation of personality, none of which can be taught in a school which deliberately rejects the teaching of morality and religion. Plato was right when he taught that the primary purpose of education is the inculcation of the distinction of right and wrong.

Parents have, perhaps unconsciously, fallen prey to the fallacy propounded by those intelligentsia who, to cover up their own reactionary theories, call themselves "progressives." This group has led parents to believe that evil, sin and crime are due to ignorance, and that if we educate by imparting knowledge we will abolish crime. Typical of this was Guizot, who when non-religious education began said: "He who opens a school, closes a prison." Today the facts retort to Guizot: "Well, we opened thousands of schools, but we closed no prisons."

> Our crime bill today is $40,000,000.00 a day.
> Our prison population has nearly doubled since 1927.
> We have the largest homicide rate in the world.
> This rate has doubled in the last thirty years.
> Our murder rate is from 6 to 40 times higher than European countries in normal times.
> A major crime is committed every 24 seconds.
> We have a murder every 40 minutes.

Never before in the history of the world was there so much knowledge; and never before so little coming to the knowledge of the Truth. Never before so much straining for life; never before so many unhappy lives. Never before so much science; never before was it used so for the destruction of human life.

In the face of this, then, shall parents not see that it is not the intellects of the world that have gone wrong; it is consciences. Reason, without moral purpose, can be reason at the service of evil as well as good. It is not the schools that are to blame; it is the parents. The right to educate belongs to them.

A final indication of the breakdown of parental authority is the present tendency of mothers who, outside of cases of necessity, work in war plants to the utter neglect and detriment of their children. In Los Angeles a social worker counted forty-five infants locked in cars at a single parking lot while their mothers were at work in war plants. In jam-packed Warren Township, outside of Detroit, children who go to school on an afternoon shift have actually been sent out to wander the streets at night so they will sleep later and not wake up their working parents early in the morning. One thirteen-year-old girl in a beer hall told the California State Department of Health officer, "I'm just waiting until twelve. My bed is not empty until then."

The root of this trouble is in the *home;* and those who talk about more nurseries, better playgrounds, curfews, better milk, and more dance halls, are perhaps diminishing the effect but not removing the cause.

Behind every delinquent child is a delinquent parent. Behind every broken young life is a broken home. There are problem children only because there are problem parents.

It therefore behooves those mothers who are doing defense work, to the utter neglect of their children, not to flatter themselves that they are aiding the war effort. The price for working in a war plant is too high, when a little less time spent in welding pipe to pipe, and a little more time spent in welding child to virtue would profit America a thousand times more. In many cases, it is not a desire to hasten victory and peace that spurs such a mother on to work, but a desire to make money. And what kind of peace will we have if, during the war, these mothers turn out future mothers with a sordid background of disease and crime? Our soldiers at the front are entitled to better wives when they return, or else the fighting is all in vain. This war's greatest casualty so far is—*the American home*.

Does this mean the American home is doomed? No! There are high hopes for better home life in the new America arising in the hearts of the soldiers. This war has brought home to the American soldier a glaring contradiction between his education and the ideas for which he is fighting. He has thus come to see that some of his peace education was wrong, and his war ideas are right.

Such statements as the following are commonly heard today: "In college I was taught that I was only an animal, but in the army I am taught to act like a man; or my professor told me that there was no difference between right and wrong, good and evil; but now my buddies die, and I prepare to die to prove that Hitler was wrong and we are right. My textbooks ridiculed sin and evil, but I find that war is caused because some men are evil. In school I was taught to be self-expressive; I was told that inhibitions and restraints were wrong, and that liberty meant to do whatever I pleased. In war I learned obedience, discipline, restraint and, above all, that any one who died to preserve that kind of eviscerated liberty was a fool. In law school I was taught that there were no inalienable rights, but on last July 4th I recalled the Declaration of Independence and realized that I was fighting to preserve those inalienable rights which my law school denied. My teachers told me that I must try to get all I can out of life, but on the battlefield I learned to give even my life."

Thus has our youth aroused himself to the tremendous disproportion between what his head was taught in school and what his heart learned amid death and shell and sweat and blood; *theoretical* repudiation of the moral law in education, and the *practical necessity* of it to win a war and establish peace.

This war has knocked into a cocked hat all those vaporous theorizings of naturalist education which separated education from morality, which understood freedom of speech as freedom from morality; freedom of religion as freedom from worship; freedom from Fascism as freedom for Communism; freedom from fear as freedom from law; and freedom of thought as freedom from truth.

The future of America is in the homes. This sounds like a platitude, but it is not, for unless the home is sound, America will not be sound. The rebirth of the home is conditioned upon three factors, all of which are grounded in the moral law:

First, marriage is a permanent bond until death. There are only two words in the vocabulary of love: "you" and "always." "You" because love is unique; "always" because love is timeless. No one ever said, "I will love you for two years and six months." The modern rubbish about sex confuses feeling with love, an organic reaction with an act of will, and falsely believes that when the "thrill" is gone, marriage is ended, forgetful that in marriage, as in running a race, there is a second wind. What the moderns call the "thrill" is only the choke that starts the motor; moderns never stay together long enough to enjoy the thrill of driving. The frosting is not the cake, but the moral law says you may not take the frosting unless you eat the cake. One of the great values of a vow is that it keeps couples together during the shock of the first cold plunge, that later on they may enjoy the swim. Love is life's courier and must not linger only in the rivers of rapture, but must launch out into the deeper and more authentic waters where the single happiness of "being together" mirrors the mystery of God's eternity and reflects the harmonies of the Triune God.

Second, marriage by its very nature is destined to bear fruit, for love is mutual self-giving which ends in self-recovery. All love is creative—even God's. All love tends to an incarnation—even God's. The spark of love, caught from the flames of Heaven's altars, was not given to scorch the flesh, but to solder life. The only reason life ever surrenders itself to life is to meet the challenge of death and conquer individual weakness by filling up the other's lacking measure in the birth of their mutual love. As the marriage of earth and tree is messianic to new life, so man and woman must not make a covenant with death but, in obedience to nature's law, pay back life's loan of life with life and not with death. In vain will they who break the lute of God's designs ever hope to snare the music. Humanity is the quarry, husband and wife the sculptors, and every child they beget a living stone to be fitted and compacted into the temple, the cornerstone of which is God.

Third, marriage can prosper only on condition of

sacrifice. All love craves a cross—even God's. True love is sacrificial. That is why courtship is characterized by gift-giving—a surrender of what one *has*. In marriage this sacrificial love should deepen by a surrender of what one *is*. Because too many measure their love for another by the pleasure which the other gives, they are in reality not in love, but in the swamps of selfishness. Hence to preserve the family, the greatest sorrow of each member should be to be outdone by the cherished rival in the least advantage of self-giving. Our poor, frail human souls at best are like jangled strings, made toneless by self-love; and not until we tighten them with self-discipline can we attune them to those harmonies that come from God, wherein each, having given to the other hostage of its heart, finds himself free in the glorious liberty of the children of God.

Peace first came to the world when the Wise Men discovered a family. And the dawn of peace will come again when other wise men return to homes where, in the new vision of domesticity, they see the human family of father, mother, and children, as the reverse order of the Holy Family: A Child, A Mother, and A Father.

CHAPTER VI

The Pillar of Freedom

THE BASIC PRINCIPLE of the Social Order is: *Freedom is a moral power, not a physical power.*

The most often used word in this World War is "Freedom," as the word most often used in the last World War was "Democracy." What the slogan "make the world safe for Democracy" was to the last World War, the phrase the "Four Freedoms" is to this. We do hope that this war does not do to the freedom of the world what the last World War did to Democracy.

It could happen that as Democracy ended in Totalitarianism in Germany, Italy and Russia, so freedom could end in slavery—unless we understand aright the nature of freedom, and how to keep it.

Freedom may be understood in either of two ways, one of which is wrong, and the other right; that is: physical freedom and moral freedom. Physical freedom is the power to do whatever you *please;* moral freedom is the right to do whatever you *ought.* I *can* do many things if I please; for example, stuff your mattress with old razor blades or turn a machine gun on your chickens; but *ought* I?

87

Physical freedom is based on *power,* either the power of the individual, as in the doctrine of Liberalism, or the power of race, nation, or class, as with the systems of Fascism, Nazism, and Communism.

Moral freedom, on the contrary, is based not on power but on the moral law of God. It envisages freedom as perfected within the law, rather than outside it, for the best self-expression is self-perfection.

Physical freedom means license, the power to draw triangles with four sides, giraffes with short necks, the power to plot against one's country and to break the commandments of God and of men, on the theory that he who restrains individual egotism restrains freedom.

Moral freedom means purchasing the right to fly by obeying the laws of gravitation, the right to drive a car by obeying the traffic laws, the right to be an American by obeying the laws of America, the right to be a child of God by obeying the moral law.

Moral freedom is upheld by men of good will, who, whether they have analyzed the concept thoroughly or not, believe in the words of the Saviour: "And the truth shall make you free," and "Where the Spirit of the Lord is, there is liberty."

It was this moral kind of freedom in a *political* form that the Greeks fought to preserve from the despotism of the Persians; it was this kind of freedom in a *spiritual* form which the Christians suffered martyrdom to preserve from the absolutism of Caesar. And it is this kind of freedom in an *international* form that we are seeking to preserve against the brutality of dictatorships.

The point we are making is that freedom is meaningless apart from the moral law. To prove it, let us glance at the Four Freedoms for which we are fighting: freedom of religion, freedom of speech, freedom from want, freedom from fear.

Not a single one of these four freedoms is an end in itself; they have meaning only in the context of the moral law of God.

(1) Why, for example, should there be freedom of religion? Because of the sacredness and inviolability of the human person, and his right to adore God according to the light of his conscience. Freedom of religion does not mean therefore the right to impose irreligion on people any more than freedom to live means the right to murder.

(2) Why should there be freedom of speech? Because speech, being an instrument, is to be used for the proper purpose of speech; that is, the communication of truth, goodness, knowledge and information; and not for the diffusion of scandals, lies, treason or immorality. Freedom of speech does not give one the right to destroy freedom of speech, any more than the right to light a match gives one the right to burn down one's neighbor's house.

(3) Why should there be freedom from want? Be-

cause the necessities and the decent comforts of life are the material conditions for the development of personality, and therefore for the salvation of the soul. Freedom from want no more gives one the right to abundance purchased by making others want than freedom to possess means freedom to dispossess.

(4) Why should there be freedom from fear? Because peace of mind is the condition of culture, and culture is impossible when a man fears either the consequences of his own sins or the consequences of the sins of others. The right to freedom from fear never means the right to terrorize others, any more than the murderer's fear of jail gives him a right to kill the judge.

Thus we are brought back to the beginning: if we destroy the moral roots of freedom we cannot expect to keep the fruits of freedom. Freedom is responsibility, not license. Freedom divorced from moral responsibility—that is, freedom divorced from God—is anarchy.

Freedom of religion will die if we shirk our responsibilities or duties to God.

Freedom of speech will die if we shirk our responsibility to truth.

Freedom from want will vanish if we shirk our responsibility to our fellowman.

Freedom from fear will vanish if we shirk our responsibility to love those who are in distress.

Four freedoms set in the moral law are therefore quite different from four freedoms isolated from it. As a matter of fact, in the latter case, they would be absolutely wicked and should be spurned, as they were by Our Blessed Lord on four occasions.

(1) Our Lord rejected a false freedom of religion. Satan appeared to Him on the mountain top, and unrolled before His mind's eye all the nations, kingdoms, and empires of the world in an increasing panorama of pomp and power, and in one of the most frightening and terrifying statements in all Scripture, Satan said: "All these will I give thee, if falling down thou wilt adore me." Here was a freedom of religion in the false sense of the term; that is, the freedom to adore either God or Satan. And Our Blessed Lord rejected it, for He would not have a freedom of religion that meant the freedom to be diabolical, anti-God, and anti-moral.

(2) Our Lord rejected a false freedom of speech. Led before one of the judges, false charges, lies, and accusations were hurled in His face. The judge offered the Divine Master a false freedom of speech: "Answerest thou nothing to the things that are laid to thy charge by these men?" But He held His peace, and would not speak, for freedom of speech ceases to be freedom of speech when speech may be used only to confirm a lie. It is the truth that makes you free—not a lie.

(3) Our Lord rejected a false freedom from want. After Our Lord fasted for forty days, Satan appeared before him and pointed to little stones that resembled in appearance Jewish bread, and suggested, "If thou be the Son of God, command that these stones be made bread." Satan, too, it seems, believes in freedom from want—but Our Lord refused to accept Satan's abundance, for it would have been purchased at the cost of disobedience to His Father's Will.

(4) Our Lord rejected a false freedom from fear. On Holy Thursday night, when Judas led a band of soldiers down to the Brook of Cedron and into the Garden to apprehend Our Divine Lord, Peter in one of his frequent impetuous moments drew a sword, and hacked off the ear of the servant of the high priest. Peter apparently believed in security or freedom from fear; but it was the wrong kind. In reprimand, Our Lord said to Peter: "Put up again thy sword into its place: for all that take the sword shall perish with the sword." No freedom from fear would the Saviour of the world have if it were purchased at the cost of injury to our fellowman.

Hence not a single one of the Four Freedoms is an end in itself. Either they are means to the attainment of moral purposes or they are evil and wicked. Freedom *from* something is meaningful only when we are free *for* something, and until we know what we want to be free *for,* there is not much use in struggling or risking our lives.

What use is freedom of religion, if there is no God to worship?

What use is freedom of speech, if there is no truth to defend?

What use is freedom from want, if such security is purchased at the cost of another's privation?

What use is freedom from fear, if such security is purchased at the cost of one's soul?

Once divorce freedom of religion from God, freedom of speech from truth, freedom from want and freedom from fear from Justice, and the Four Freedoms will become the Four Horsemen of the Apocalypse riding roughshod over the world in Satanic fury, trampling out every freedom on earth except the glorious freedom to be a martyr for the glory of God who made us free.

This being true, these corollaries of freedom follow from the moral law:

First: When we affirm the Four Freedoms, we must not assume that we can give freedom to the enslaved peoples of Europe. All we can do is to remove *external* hindrance to freedom.

Freedom is from the spirit, not from power. We can no more give Europe freedom than we can give a European a soul. All we can do is to say that the European's moral freedom shall not be inhibited by external compulsions. You can lead a horse to water, but you cannot make him drink. You can lead the enslaved masses of Europe to the fountains of the four liberties, but they will not drink unless in their souls *they choose* to be free with the glorious liberty of the children of God. Freedom is in the inner *will*, not in external power. That is why no power on earth can make men free.

In order to be free, each man must make a pact with his soul. Let us not then promise to the enslaved peoples of Europe something we cannot deliver. They have already been deceived too much. Communism promised freedom through economic abundance, and gave them spiritual starvation; Nazism promised them freedom through *lebensraum* and gave them *totesraum;* Fascism promised them freedom through law, but gave them law without freedom. Democracy must not add to this tragic litany by promising a freedom which only God can give. We are not God, and we cannot give God's gifts. We enjoy God's liberty, but we do not create it. All that we can promise is this: "We will take the shackles off your legs so you can walk out of prison and· get down on your knees and remake your soul! We will make you *freed* men, but only God can make you *free* men." More than that we cannot say without blasphemy.

We are *born* free! "And the tribune coming, said to

him: Tell me. Art thou a Roman? But he said: Yea.
And the tribune answered: I obtained the being free of
this city with a great sum. And Paul said: But I was
born so. Immediately therefore they departed from him
that were about to torture him. The tribune also was
afraid after he understood that he was a Roman citizen
and because he had bound him."

Second: Freedom is not an heirloom which originally
belonged to the Founding Fathers of our country and
which has been passed down to us from generation to
generation ever since. Freedom is rather an endowment
like life, which is preserved by resisting from time to
time the challenge of disease and death.

The freedom that Washington won for us has not
come down to us as an antique. Freedom for those days
is not necessarily freedom for ours, unless we win it
too, as they did—by sacrifice, fire and tears.

A freedom that costs nothing is worth nothing. Freedom, like a tree, needs to be quickened and refreshed
now and then by the blood of patriots and the dew of
self-sacrificing citizens. It is not only the original cost
of freedom that is high; it is the upkeep.

Freedom therefore is not foolproof; it demands restraint, law and discipline. Therefore it will never
mean the right to abuse Justice, to spurn Mercy, and
to ignore Truth. Set within the moral law, freedom
must always be strong enough to preserve freedom.

Finally, freedom is ours only to give away. Every man may give his freedom away, either to creatures, to public opinion or to God. The creature to which he surrenders his freedom may be money, or power or a human being —for all love is slavery, seeking to unburden itself for the object of its affection.

Others give up their freedom to the moods and opinions of the moment, and they are legion. Swayed by the winds of every commentator and propagandist, they have no judgments of their own, no standards of their own; and thus, while mouthing slogans of liberty, they surrender the last vestige of it to a slavery worse than chains, for here the mind is bound.

Finally, others give up freedom to God, wanting nothing, seeking nothing, desiring nothing except to do His Will in all things, in a slavery to Perfect Life, Perfect Truth, Perfect Love, which ends in the highest kind of freedom; for to "serve Him is to rule."

There is not a man alive who does not make one of these three surrenders! And of the three, only the last makes freedom eternal, for "if . . . the son of God shall make you free, you shall be free indeed."

CHAPTER VII

The Pillar of World Unity

THE BASIC PRINCIPLE of the international order is: *The world is one because it was made by one Lord and is governed by His moral law.*

All men are one because God made man. Paul, a Jew, standing on the hill of the Areopagus, declared this great truth to the Senators of Greece: "God . . . hath made of one, all mankind, to dwell upon the whole face of the earth." And then, as if to remind them that this was not the teaching of his people alone, he quoted for them Aratus and Cleathus, saying: "As some also of your poets said: *For we are also his offspring.*"

The world became united only in those periods of history in which men recognized the overlordship of God. It was because the pagan, Cyrus, recognized that he was but an instrument in the hands of the God of Israel that he could bring himself to respect the rights of a conquered people and order rebuilt for them their Temple at Jerusalem. Alexander the Great is quoted by Plutarch as saying: "God is the common father of all men." No wonder then that he ordered that every city and every state should open its gates to the exiled opponents of the party and that his own officers should take brides from among the conquered people. And who shall forget Cicero's words that "the universe is to be regarded as a single commonwealth, since all are subject to the heavenly law and divine intelligence of Almighty God."

These dim aspirations of pre-Christian times were but feeble echoes of the Hebrew truth that God "shall be called the God of the whole earth." All of them were but dim foreshadowings of the day when the whole world would be enrolled, when the King of Kings and the Lord of Lords should be born—Creator of all men, Redeemer who made all men one because of all men. How much wiser the pre-Christian pagan was than our post-Christian pagan! Shall those of us who have forgotten the wisdom of the ancient pagans, the revelation of the Jews, and the sublime truths of Christianity, think that we can build One World on any other foundation? To unite men there must be something outside men, just as to tie up a bundle of sticks there must be some one outside the sticks. A moral law outside of nations to which all nations can appeal, and to which they must submit even when the decision goes against them, is the only condition of world peace. That is why we say there will never be one world until we all learn to pray, *"Our Father,* who art in Heaven."

The only alternative to One World based on One

Lord and one moral law is to have many worlds and many lords, where each nation is its own law, its own god. Like the workers on the Tower of Babel, each of us will then speak a different language and live by a different code. Having naught in common, the project of world peace must, like the Tower, be abandoned. In that case, there would be no way to decide whether Japanese atrocities were wrong and American humanitarianism right, except by a war between these gods in which might decides what is right. To all who have eyes it should be as clear as the stones in the road that the day we make a Godless world we make also a loveless world.

There were 4,568 treaties of peace signed before the League of Nations between the two World Wars, and two hundred and eleven in the nine months before this war broke out. Only the smaller fraction of them were kept. What great change in the heart of man has taken place since 1939 to make us believe that from now on treaties and pledges will be kept? Have our souls been reborn? Let us be realistic about it! Why should any treaty be kept under the present set-up of the world? What is the source of their obligation? Is the obligation rooted in God and conscience, or in convenience, strategy, or force? It is either Right or Might. It is just as simple as that, for *no treaty creates its own obligation*. Obligation is outside the treaty, or else there is no obligation. In such a case, *either an obligation does not exist or its basis is force.*

This moral principle that we can have One World only on condition of one law breaks immediately with the commonly accepted principle that (because no city in the world is more than sixty hours from an airport) the world is one. It should be obvious to anyone who has lived through two World Wars in twenty-one years that rapid communications have the same potentialities for destruction as they have for unity. An airplane in itself is indifferent as to whether it scatters flowers or bombs. Unity depends therefore not on communications but on the singleness of purpose for which communications are used.

This brings us back to the antiphon that has been ringing through these chapters. "We must gather together the hearts of all those who are magnanimous and upright in a solemn vow not to rest until in all peoples and all the nations of the earth a vast legion shall be formed, bent on bringing society back to its center of gravity which is the law of God."

What are some corollaries of the moral law as applied to the international order? The moral law in its application to the world must provide a new international order with five characteristics: It must be positive, juridical, realistic, single in purpose and uncompromising.

The Unity of Nations for the defeat of barbarism

must not be negative, but positive; that is, it must not
be grounded on the common hatred of an aggressor
but on the acceptance of common moral principles.
Military unity does not necessarily mean political unity.
The two are commonly confused. Gratitude for military
cooperation does not oblige us to go into ecstasies about
the political ideology of any foreign power. The fire-
men who put out the fire in your home render a negative help, but they never help rebuild your home. In
like manner, it is not the defeat of a particular barbarism which makes us true allies, but rather the agreement that a temple of peace can be built only on the
foundation of the moral order and with the stone of
justice and the cement of love.

The new international order must be juridical. The
moral law forbids any nation to satisfy its selfish am-
bitions or imperialistic aims by violating the sovereignty
of other nations, independently of a judicial process
and before the court convenes. Therefore, no signatory
of a declaration of united peace may settle international
questions unilaterally, by force, independently of the
moral judgment of other nations. Justice becomes a
farce if a thief is permitted to say to the court: "I will
permit you to hear my case only on condition that I
keep my loot."

The new international order must be realistic. The
moral law realistically affirms that no one can give that

which he has not. Therefore any nation which does not give freedom of religion, freedom of speech, and freedom of press to its own citizens, can hardly be counted on, in a society of nations, to give to other peoples those rights which its own citizens do not enjoy.

In the new international order there must be singleness of purpose. The moral law admits of no double standard. Non-belligerency is right in certain circumstances, but it is wrong when purchased at the cost of morality. No one more strongly condemned appeasement of the strong powers who were violating the sovereignty of other nations than Marshal Stalin who, speaking to England and America in 1939, said: "England and America let Germany have Austria, despite the undertaking to defend her independence; they let her have the Sudeten region; they abandoned Czechoslovakia to her fate, thereby violating all her obligations. . . . Far be it from me to moralize on the policy of non-intervention, to talk of treason, treachery, and so on. It would be naïve to preach morals to people who recognize no human morality." Stalin here hailed America and England before the bar of justice and condemned them for appeasing Germany when it violated the sovereignty of the Sudeten, Austria, and Czechoslovakia. Would it not then be equally wrong for us to appease another foreign power if it violated the sovereignty of other lands in the same manner?

The morality of an action is not decided by *who* violates, but by what is violated. Would it not be wrong for America to invade Canada on the basis of mutual assistance pacts and incorporate it into our republic? Was it not wrong for Germany to do that with Czechoslovakia? Then what makes it right when another foreign power does it? Unless we defend moral rights when they needs must be defended, we may get into that state described by Shakespeare:

> Now, as fond fathers,
> Having bound up the threatening twigs of birch,
> Only to stick it in their children's sight
> For terror, not to use, in time the rod
> Becomes more mock'd than fear'd; so our decrees
> Dead to infliction, to themselves are dead,
> And liberty plucks justice by the nose.*

The new international order, finally, must be uncompromising. The moral integrity of a nation depends on fidelity to its pledges. In the Atlantic Charter we pledged (1) "No aggrandizement, territorial or other"; (2) "No territorial changes that do not accord with the freely expressed wishes of the people concerned"; (3) "All nations of the world must come to the abandonment of the use of force."

No other joint declaration was ever as specific as this, nor did any other so unify men of good will behind

* *Measure for Measure*, Act I, Scene 3.

the war effort. If America ever sacrifices that charter for any temporary benefit or appeasement, it will not regain the good will of the people within a generation. It is therefore a shock to read this editorial in a metropolitan newspaper: "We must find out what Russia wants in payment for her fight, and we must be realistic about it. If Russia wants, as is now supposed, something like the old Czarist boundaries—including Finland, Latvia, Lithuania, Estonia, and a large chunk of Poland—we had better concede to her wishes, rather than stick to the Atlantic Charter." Another metropolitan newspaper states that "if Russia wants Poland, it is far better to give up Poland than to offend Russia." By the same logic, why not give up the Philippines rather than offend Japan? Why, in other words, is Russia right in doing the very same thing which Stalin said was wrong when Hitler invaded Austria, the Sudeten region, and Czechoslovakia?

Herein lies America's greatest danger—paralysis of spirit, refusal to stand up for the right regardless of consequences. We will never be conquered from without; no one can conquer us but ourselves. Never will we be murdered! But America can commit suicide! Other nations may sentence her to die, but America alone can be the executioner. It will never be invaded by armies; but it can be pervaded by a supine submission to evil! Our frontiers are safe; our inner defense can be betrayed only by what is false within! As Lincoln said: "At what point then is the approach of danger to be expected? I answer, if it ever reaches us it must spring from amongst us; it cannot come from abroad. If destruction be our lot, we must ourselves be its author and finisher. As a nation of free men, we must live through all times, or die by suicide. . . . Many free countries have lost their liberty, and ours may lose hers; but if she shall, be it my proudest plume, not that I was the last to desert, but that I never deserted her."

We have had political expressions of the moral law in the Atlantic Charter, in the Four Freedoms and in the following magnificent words of the State Department, which makes one feel proud of being American. They were written in defense of Latvia, Estonia and Lithuania: "The United States will continue to stand by these principles of sovereignty because of the conviction of the American people that unless the doctrine in which these principles are inherent once again governs the relations between nations—the rule of reason, of justice and of law—the basis of modern civilization cannot be preserved."

These declarations are in the great tradition of Washington, who reminds us that religion and morality are the indispensable pillars of good government. Because Americans generally accept the moral and religious basis of an international order, they are embarrassed by attacks on religion, whether official or unofficial. Some, inspired by the best of sentiments, protest against such attacks on the ground that those who make them forget that politics is separate from religion, and that it hurts international relations to confuse them. This criticism is based on a nineteenth-century attitude which no longer fits the twentieth-century facts. During the nineteenth century religion and politics established a kind of *modus vivendi,* or tacit agreement not to interfere in the other's domain. It was an arrangement like unto a husband and wife who lived peaceably so long as the husband stayed out of the kitchen.

But what actually happened was that while religion was staying in the parlor, irreligion, the next-door neighbor, came in and stole the political wife. In other words, while politics asked religion not to interfere, politics became irreligious, first with the Communists, then with the Fascists, and finally with the Nazis. That is why the Church condemned all three. And the Church condemned these three ideologies not because they were bad political systems, but because they were bad religions. In other words, the new politics *is* a religion. Nothing today is secular. The temporal smothers the spiritual.

This war is therefore more a religious war than it is a nationalistic war. It is a conflict between two totally different philosophies of life. Never before in the his-

tory of Christianity has the cause of God and Man, of
Religion and Freedom, been as nearly identical as it is
at this very hour. As Joan of Arc fought simultaneously
for the Kingdom of God and for France, so America
is fighting, in an analogical sense, for a political idea
which is essentially a *moral* ideal.

The tragedy of attacks on religion within our own
camp is not that they may endanger our military suc-
cess, but that they reveal a disparity of ideals—as different as night and day. There is therefore not much
point in reminding the enemies of religion that religion
and politics are separate, because to them politics *is
religion* in the sense that politics is anti-religious, and
admits of no other law or code or morality than itself.

From quite another point of view there is such a
thing as looking at such disturbances of the international moral order through the eyes of faith.

There is nothing new in this world. There are only
the same old things happening to new people. The
Gospel is the pre-history of the Church. No sword is
lifted against Christ's Church but that Christ feels the
wound. Of each new agony and woe, He can say: "My
pain, My grief, My death." Hence, when I read of
attacks launched against religion, I remember that they
happened before. I go back to the Gospels, and as if it
were an eternal newspaper I read the old news that is
eternally new.

If I hear it said that the Church is opposed to the freedom-loving peoples of the world, and that there can be no peace in Europe until religion is crushed, somehow or other my mind immediately begins to think of the day that the Son of the Most High was standing in the sunlit balustrade of the Fortress Antonia, and the same charges were hurled against Him. "We have found this man perverting our nation, and forbidding to give tribute to Caesar, and saying that He is Christ the King." That was a roundabout way, in those less clever days of name-calling, of saying that He was a Fascist. They were all lies! But what difference does it make? Did not Hitler say, "You can never get people to believe little lies, but you can get them to believe big ones"? But though the dictator boasts of his power, the words of the Saviour still ring above him in a message of hope: "You would not have this power unless it were given to you from above."

Then when I hear the enemies of religion say the Church is hated—hated in Belgium, in France, in Italy, in Holland, in Great Britain and the United States—I remember how well Our Lord foretold that this day would come to pass. "If the world hate you, know ye that it hath hated me before you. If you had been of the world, the world would love its own; but because you are not of the world, but I have chosen you out of the world, therefore the world hateth you. . . . If they have persecuted me, they will also persecute you."

He was hated too! Once there echoed in His ears the final shout of those who said, "Crucify Him, Crucify Him." Who cried for His death? The masses! Every one! But who moved the masses to hate? The leaders, the ancients, the makers of public opinion. In the simple language of the Gospel: "They. persuaded the people." St. Matthew here reads like today's newspaper—the people are still being persuaded!

Now as then, like its Master, the Church is caught between two political fires which are themselves at war. Just as the Christ was buffeted between Pilate and Herod, who hated one another, so the Church is attacked by those who hate one another, by its Pilates who regard the Church as a political menace, and by the Herods who regard the Church as a political fool.

Conscience has always been defenseless before power, and Justice made ridiculous before the imperial impulses!

But what a terrible, ending to the story: so simply stated—"And Herod and Pilate were made friends, that same day."

It was the one thing on which they could agree—a common dictational hatred of Divine Love!

How shall we know whether the world will make a peace grounded on the moral law? By what test shall we recognize fidelity to the Atlantic Charter? The test is Poland. Poland is a cameo, not a piece in the mosaic of nations. Poland is not an aspect of the international problem; it is the international problem in miniature. Whatever happens to Poland will happen to the world. If we fail to sustain the moral law in this test, then, since there is a God in the heavens, we may expect this war to be followed by an interregnum of barbarism, and that in turn by World War III.

The disintegration of any civilization, or a crisis in history, bears within it the threat of an interregnum of barbarism. As in the physical order the putrid remains of the unburied dead create a pestilence, so the disintegration of the liberal civilization through which we have just lived, and which was strong only because it was a parasite on Christianity, creates the possibility of chaos. Liberalism left to itself is really only a transition between a culture which was Christian and one which will be anti-Christian.

By barbarism we mean the destruction of moral values, or the repudiation of the funded heritage of culture. The barbarism of the new era will not be like that of the Huns of old; it will be technical, scientific, secular, and propagandized. It will come not from without, but from within, for barbarism is not *outside* us; it is *underneath* us. Older civilizations were destroyed by imported barbarism; modern civilization breeds its own.

A high government official has told us to expect the loss of 500,000 men. That is not too high a price to pay for justice, honor and peace. But if these deaths, like that of Simeon, do not point to the salvation of the world, then their souls, like ghosts, will arise to haunt us in the night. No material profit, no conquest of any land, no crushing of any particular barbarities, can justify such crimson rivers, unless they purchase for us the greatest intangibles and imponderables of all: justice, peace and freedom.

Our hope for the reign of the moral law must be in prayer. Pray for the world, for the Church, for the enemies of the Church. What happens between you and God when you are on your knees is of vital significance for the world. Pray for Russia! Ever since 1929 all the priests all over the world and all the Catholics who attend daily Mass say the prayers at the end of Low Mass for the intention of Russia. Dostoevsky foretold of his own country that after it had passed through a diabolical anti-God stage it would sit at the feet of Christ and learn His Gospel. To the dawn of that day our eyes expectantly look wherein nations can live in one world because there is one moral law and one Lord.

These are hard days for the Church. All that it is trying to do today is to preserve the negatives of a moral order as warring nations tear up the photograph. It is no more interested in political regimes than was its Divine Master.

Christ in His Church rides through the world not